What a fresh, original voice! Melody Newey Johnson's poems look inward and outward at the same time and therefore sing with insights about her journey through the canyons, fields, and mountains of a well-lived, thoughtful life. Her metaphors illustrate this simultaneity: her belly is "a moon full of baby"; she trusts the sky's "billion years of blue." Poems as tight and spare as Emily Dickinson's offer the same kind of depth: beneath each carefully cut, honed surface lie extraordinary thought, faith, and imagination for readers to follow.

—Susan Elizabeth Howe
Author of *Stone Spirits* and *Salt*,
and an AML Award-winner in poetry

Perched somewhere between George Herbert and Mary Oliver, Melody Newey Johnson's poems offer a sustained celebration of "heaven in ordinary." These poems quietly and gently fold experience in on itself, bringing out the richness that had slipped our view even though it had been there all along.

—Jason Kerr
Assistant Professor of English
Brigham Young University

Christ's broken body wrapped in a linen chrysalis. Childbirth: a miracle startling as the Nile turned to blood. A collision with modernity, shattering as a motorcycle crash. Melody Newey Johnson's *An Imperfect Roundness* shows us God in life's earthquakes, fires, and stillnesses.

—James Goldberg
Author of *The Five Books of Jesus*
and *Remember the Revolutions*

AN IMPERFECT
ROUNDNESS

BY COMMON CONSENT PRESS is a non-profit publisher dedicated to producing affordable, high-quality books that help define and shape the Latter-day Saint experience. BCC Press publishes books that address all aspects of Mormon life. Our mission includes finding manuscripts that will contribute to the lives of thoughtful Latter-day Saints, mentoring authors and nurturing projects to completion, and distributing important books to the Mormon audience at the lowest possible cost.

AN IMPERFECT ROUNDNESS

POEMS

MELODY NEWEY JOHNSON

BCC PRESS

For information contact
By Common Consent Press
4062 S. Evelyn Dr.
Salt Lake City, UT 84124-2250

Cover design: D Christian Harrison
Book design: Andrew Heiss

www.bccpress.org
ISBN-13: 978-1-948218-29-0

10 9 8 7 6 5 4 3 2 1

For my children:
Lauren, Luke, Sara, Daniel, Eric, Aimee,
and for my grandchildren— born and yet to be.

Contents

Holy Water

Be Still

Amazing Grace

Music & Silence

Preface

This collection explores the lived experience of womanhood, motherhood, aging, loss, and healing, through spiritual inquiry grounded in faith and in the natural world. God appears everywhere within these pages, but not always in the form one might expect. Mormon references abound, for those familiar with my faith tradition. Yet, I hope the poems appeal to believers in any spiritual practice and, more broadly, to anyone with imagination and a desire to see the magic and divine in everyday moments.

From among a larger family of works, these particular poems organically congregated, then spread themselves along a meandering pathway of understanding. Individual poems provide a pause on the path, serving as meditations or devotional pieces. Collectively, I see them as a spiritual memoir— verses spanning a lifetime— both in their ordering within the manuscript and in the compositional timeline. Some poems were composed decades ago, when I was a young mother of small children. Others emerged from a fresh, middle-of-life marriage.

Though perhaps not initially crafted for communal consumption, they seem to want to be shared, especially now, in a time of a global health crisis. May this book offer you peace, hope, and a bit of wonder, dear reader, wherever you are in the world and in your life's journey.

— Melody

Last Night I Prayed

I want this   *life*
to be easy.

God said:
It is.

Genesis

"Nourish beginnings. Not all things are blest, but the seeds of all things are blest. The blessing is in the seed."

—Muriel Rukeyser

An Imperfect Roundness

This morning a
lopsided moon
hangs low
in the sky,
heavy with
a new day

like my belly—
a moon
full of baby,
an imperfect
roundness, heavy
with hope.

Newborn Hymn

I know your scent before they
lay you on my breast, your voice
before you breathe warm in
my ear: Those sounds
you make as you make
your way toward life

the way you reach for air,
your almostcry, the squeak and
uhmah, uhmah, uhmmm.
You speak in strange,
familiar wordless tones—
it's like you're singing.

Come Now

to this

one life
one voice

and days enough
to sing all the music

heaven wrote
in you.

Nativity

for the December child

There were no wise men come
when my child was born,
ten days before the holy one.

There was no star,
no bleating sheep
no one traveled far.

But there was an angel,
spoke of light and love—
my newborn son like hers
brought hope.

Maybe It's You

You ask me for evidence of God,
proof of divine intervention
like things you read in the bible—

> a red River Nile,
> lepers healed
> the dead brought back

I'm not sure what to say except:
consider your own creation

> fire and heat, the whirlwind

the violent hours before
you erupted into the world—

> earthquakes, the great flood

ask your mother, she was there
she'll tell you about it and

about redemption too—
the impossible light you brought

> the rainbow

and how the wounds of
a hundred generations
were healed with your coming.

Divine
Origins

Mother wisdom

```
s                    s
o                    t
l                    r
a                    e
c                    n
e                    g
                     t
     Father truth    h
```

God Is A Farmer's Wife

She's been awake since five because it's her nature
and breakfast will be ready when you come.

She knows every recipe by heart.

She knows the sound of your feet moving down the hall
toward the kitchen across those few creaky boards,

knows your sister and brother's sound too
because every footfall bears witness of its own.

She is warm and round and strong and when she
speaks, the sun begins to rise. She wakes it for you.

Yesterday she plowed fields and fed horses in the
middle of the day while you slept because you were tired.

When the time comes to dream yourself away from this place
she won't forget the sound of your feet, your quiet breathing.

When you go, she'll bless your skin to remember the warm,
round sun, your mind to recall the smell of earth; even if

you forget the plow, even if the ground is too hard.
She wants you to go, find your way, to learn the

way horses whinny, each in their own voice; you'll
breathe their sweet aroma up close: no two alike.

She knows them like she knows you.

And she knows the ground they cover when they run,
every steep, every valley. She hears them when she sleeps.

She hears the grain as it grows to feed them, the music
it makes, brushing the palms of your hands when you

pass through before or after quail who run unseen below.
And your hips— she knows how the grain flicks against them

like a horse's tail. She wants you to listen for her in
whinny and hoof, in tail-swish and quail-scurry;

to taste the song the chick would have sung, if it hadn't
been made into scrambled eggs for your breakfast.

She wants you to remember her soft apron, how the colors
stay bright even after infinite wearings in the kitchen or at the plow.

She won't miss you when you're gone because you are never gone—
the floor still squeaks where your feet found their hold in the morning

your feet, when they were soft and barely awake.

Hope & Sorrow

*"Earth has no sorrow
heaven cannot heal."*

—*Attrib. Thomas Moore*

Coming Up For Air

I.
My sister may not win her war with cancer.
When she speaks I hear the surf begin to roar,
the tide inside threatens to push me over.
Diving beneath the surface, I search for
words— perfect orbs of comfort, glowing
iridescent inside crusted shells—
I'll gather, string them tidy, together . . .
but I lose my breath, come back up for air.

II.
My mother dies, her life unstrung.
Before she leaves I think I have all
the answers: the truth of how she lived,
why she stopped. Kneeling by the bed
I hear echoes of her voice, whispers from
a velvet box: *What you know is smaller
than a pearl. The truth is an endless sea.*

III.
My son marries his love. I buy the
only strand of pearls I've ever owned.
In the middle of a desert, I feel the
ocean against my breast, a hundred
little suns rise in the palm of
my hand. I let go my grown child,
hold on to these drops of light.

Faith Crisis: Prayer

Angels carried him through air,
laid him soft against the curb
when a car hit his motorcycle
and he lifted off toward heaven.

A miracle, the paramedics said,
he flew forty feet then walked away—
forty feet of hang time
forty years in the wilderness
forty days in the desert.

His personal lent:
a clavicle and that bike
broken. He gave them up,
gained a second chance.

Now, his soul crashes into
dogma, history hidden
behind simulated smiles,
convenient community—
please, God, send angels,
give him a soft landing

Fish Bones

Unwilling to go hungry, I stave
cravings the moment they arise—
rise from chair, move toward food,
drink, whatever satisfies.

I no longer savor the sanctity of an
empty bowl or see roundness in
fish bones on black stones of
an ancient lakebed.

Have I forgotten the call of
shepherds wizened with want,
famished, looking for lost lambs?
Give me strength to stop—

listen to what hunger tells:
I have lost what feeds me,
replaced it with a notion:
I am not good enough,

smart enough, rich enough.
I am hungry for my self
and fill my belly with
everything else.

Winter heard me call your name

but the air was thick with smell
of rotting honeydew the night
my child lay ill and dying.

You wrapped me in your sweater.
I believed you for a moment when
you said everything would be all right.

       The moon covered her face in ash.

With morning, spring was gone.
I stayed cold indoors, you
made angels in the snow.

We Cross A Bridge

Grief runs swift
beneath   our   feet from
past to future
and   once or twice it
swells the banks   when
we look down   and are
swept away   or almost
but not quite.

First Vision

If prophets saw a light descend,
why do I fear the grove?
Why avoid the blinding light
or spend summers
chasing thunderheads?

Perhaps the grove is
around the next bend and
I must walk away from this
carefully constructed house
for a quiet place to kneel.

Unfinished Business

When you see the bedroom door ajar
you may think you hear a small voice behind it
inviting you to pray as you did when you
were a child: to a God both real and magic.

Remember how you knelt beside the bed on
knees bruised from child's play and didn't hurt,
how Sunday school songs were prayers
you didn't know you were singing?

Remember how you knew then without knowing:
Love is the best reason to wake up and go outside.

Like Hannah

I don't recall making a bargain,
a promise to give her back
after twenty-one years.

A mother should know:
Though formed of our flesh,
daughters were never ours to keep.

But it seems God owes me something—
some solace or recompense for
surrendering my heart with my
child when the call comes.

I put her on a plane for Fiji, give her
to the care of her Rightful Parents.
The letter says for eighteen months,
but I know better.

Law Of The Harvest

I curl myself around
warm food in my belly—
ancient, first and only comfort.

       I'm supposed to be rejoicing,
       sending my son into fields of white
       all ready to harvest. Instead,

on sky blue sheets, my heart
tumbles out of my sickled chest,
sends hope and sorrow to heaven

where the sower of all
good seeds plants my tears
for future reaping.

There's A Crack In Kenya

Mother wakes me early before the sun to tell me
about fractures. I think she says *fractions* and I say
I don't give even one-third-of-a-damn, I just want to sleep.

But she won't let it go. Kenya, she says. You know,
that place where everything started? Isn't that where
they found Lucy, the first human? That was Ethiopia, mom.

And I think you mean Eve. She was the first human.
The Bible got it wrong. Adam came later. (This is my version
of Genesis, if the stories had been told by women.)

She doesn't know what to say, but the crack has grown so wide
we're both pretty sure even Jesus or all the king's men can't put it
back together again and, anyway, mom's arms look tired.

I ask her to climb in. She tells me I'm cracked, then slides
beside me, her tired legs resting on those soft, old flannel
sheets she always makes the bed with when I come home.

She scratches my back as I roll over and we argue (laugh)
about religion and science. I'll tell you about a crack—
that day your dad moved out! She says it was like the

Gulf of Mexico washed through and made everything
verdant and new. It was like the Grand Canyon opened up
in the living room, then cool, clean air blew through this place.

You could almost hear the little burros, their hooves clicking on hardwood, and nobody ever got thirsty, even with all the wind.

I wonder if it's hot in Kenya, she says. And do they have clean water?

Holy Water

*"There will come soft rains
and the smell of the ground,
with swallows circling in
their shimmering sound ..."*

—Sara Teasdale

Sabbath-Keeping

Just so you know:
when you pass by
early Sunday morning
as I bend and kneel
over flowerbeds
trowel in hand—

this is communion,
meditation, reunion.
Perhaps next time you
will join me, bow your
head and listen with me
for God's word in soil.

Tree of Life

I make my way from great
and spacious building
pulled by love to cross
the river of darkness alone.

You glance sideways from
that straight and narrow,
leave the path, kneel,
patient for the moment
when my face turns up,
lungs scorched with new air,
when I see you there
(knees wet, hands muddied)
and you raise me from water.

No vision of the future
or end of journey: Today,
you are the tree, the fruit.

Women

the magic
ones—

the ones
who keep

the world
from dying.

Dear God,

are you invisible
because I am in you?

                        amniotic air
                        placental soil

Are my dreams the
movement you feel at night?

Are these words
our shared blood?

Heavenly Mother

I hear her best
when the rain stops

        the quiet after
        thunderstorms

when everyone
and everything

sighs in
unison.

Inland

The ocean came in this morning on
a gust of wind. A thousand miles
inland, it lapped against foothills of
the Rockies. Now, seagulls are crying,
calling for their mother. Now, a memory
of my children tasting salted sand
takes me out with the receding tide.

First Snow: God

In winter: your face,
your silver crown on

falling crystals:
words of wisdom
made solid

something to
hold on to just
long enough to

look up again and
listen for your voice.

It Hasn't Fallen On Us Yet

When fear mongers

shout warnings

I look up at a

billion years

of blue

and trust

the

sky.

Afternoon Nap With Summer Rain

drops begin to fall

I stay outside

move a little deeper

beneath the tree.

Rain Is What Matters

(as dew from heaven)

gentle
peaceful
clean cool
clarity falling singly
distilled through time and
space. Water spilled whispers
out of heaven gifts given freely
without constraint devoid of cost.
Blessings sprinkled bestowed in
transparent spheres. Multitudes of
sometime silent small things
drop by drop anointing
tiny by tiny telling
truth.

Be Still

"I have often wondered whether especially those days when we are forced to remain idle are not precisely the days spent in the most profound activity."

—Rainer Maria Rilke

Jesus

my
one word
prayer.

How It Works

You will be healed
but first
you will be
wounded.

You will be saved
but first you
will know
you are lost.

Faith, Hope, Clarity

(nighttime in the desert)

I look up
into star-cut
blueblack sky

after creeping
the car down
gravel road
and think:

It's good to
know comfort
in darkness,

to find peace on
the edges of light.

Fall Down

The preacher says in the end we'll fall
down at the Lord's feet, our garments
rent, His garment red with our blood.

If there is a judgment day it is
here now, in the moment we
see god in the unshaven man
on the curb with a whiskey bottle

or the woman with fishnet stockings
and bruises. We tell ourselves we
know who is chosen, who is chaff.
We are all beggars, every one.

Things Not Written

no letters
scratched on
paper napkins

no words spoken
into a recording
device for later

some things
are saved only
in memory

like that woman
with no teeth
eating Mongolian

barbecue
so fervently
so silent.

Waiting for Words

Magi from the East move
toward peace, their tales
retold in beams of moonlight

while I walk ancient roads alone
watching dust blow away
toward Bethlehem ...

still, still in the long dark
I hear a lullaby, lift my eyes
hoping for a wise star.

Where Is The Stone?

What has

become of

post and beam,

of the forgiven few who hung you there?

Where is the stone, the napkin, the doubter?

Where is

anything

anyone who

touched

you then?

And does it

matter

tonight

while your

voice fills

my heart

pulses

through

veins

beneath

blood

moon.

Chrysalis

Three days of white
       threads wound
       fine
       around
       around.

Three days of light
       shrouded linen
       fine
       white
       light woven.

Three days of . . .

       Where hast thou laid him?

And she thought,
Are his wings still wet?

when he said,
Touch me not.

Be Still

(a psalm)

Come to the temple of silence,
away from sounds of weary want,
from the grinding, tearing of time.

Come away from shouting daylight,
find me in the stillness of afternoon,
your ordinary afternoon.

Put down your swords,
your plowshares; take up
my burden, quiet, easy.
Carry it beneath your arm
with flute and mandolin.
Carry it in your heart, beside
memories of your mother and
apple red trees in summer.

Whisper my name, then listen.
Listen, perhaps for a very long time
or only for a heartbeat.

And I will tell you who I am,
who you are, and show you where
we meet: in you, the holy place.

Amazing Grace

"That love is all there is,
is all we know of love."

—*Emily Dickinson*

Mustard Seed

Love was always
over the next rise

until I stopped

and asked God
to move mountains.

A Valentine From God

Be an observer
of your own life

be both
sun and flower

find me
in everything

let Love be
your favorite teacher.

You began as
a curve, a comma
in your mother's womb

now unfurl yourself
let fingers open wide

then hold
someone's hand

tell the whole world
about it.

Beloved

If there is
a difference

between laughing
and flying

you're the one
to teach me.

Last Night I Dreamed

sounds of silk
smell of jasmine

taste of gold leaf
like sacrament on
my tongue when

I turned my face
toward love.

Two Angels Help A Woman Open Her Heart

descend in whispers

slip fingers through ribs to

find the place where soft bones

bend the way of love then

pull and leave her gaping

gasping born

again.

Making Ready

White pleats,
relaxed from
years of ritual use
disappear in
wash water.

Today I press them
sharp as light,
new as morning
while, in my mind,
my grandmother
hums Amazing Grace.

Love Is A Paper Crane

One morning after rain
you lay together listening
as birds chirp and bathe

you realize what began
in two dimensions—
(perfect in its simplicity)

has folded back on itself
creased by careful words
pressed with passion

into three dimensions—
love has become more
than you envisioned

when you first lifted it
from the shelf and laid it
on the fine wood table.

Music & Silence

*"When you love the world
you hear celestial music."*

—Louise Glück

One Eternal Round

and love is where we begin with seed and sun and earth and rain and moon and stars and warmth and time

Seasons
change
themselves

and
me.

Windmills

When I was a child my muscles tensed
then sprang like new rubber bands.
I won ribbons in the fifty and hundred-yard dash.
In fourth grade they called me Spider Legs—
long, lean, sprouting new hair, I moved
like lightning across playgrounds.

Today my limbs feel tired, worn out;
middle-aged thighs are dimpled, but
hungry for blue ribbons, asphalt, kickball.
I miss that familiar stretch to first base
when I was a windmill of arms and legs,
the softball a tornado touching down in my glove.

More Than This. And Less.

I say I'm plump which may be true.
I am also the slender ten-year-old
with legs so long, boys couldn't hit
me with the red rubber dodgeball
on concrete with painted yellow lines.

I say I am bothered by a large
roll of belly around my middle
this first year of second marriage,
but I also love the round
soft everywhere I've become.

My lover's hands move across
this roundness with such devotion,
adoration, I can do nothing but love
as he does this new self. I am
always more than this. And less.

Every shape I've ever been,
each silhouette—a gift from
the life of flesh. (Remember when I
grew babies and breasts so full
I didn't recognize myself?)

Today I am fuller. I see it in the photo
where we stand near Mayan ruins.
Today I am one of many shapes,
other selves, hidden within this
faithful and forgiving skin.

Picking Raspberries

Maybe I should feel guilty
for red juice on fingers,
pink stains on lips,
for so many left uneaten.

Maybe birds will find them
or sun will dry them into
tiny buds of fruit leather
(do snails eat raspberries?)

Every day after work,
I gather warm handfuls
from canes on the
south side of our home,

tumble them into mouth,
leave the rest untouched,
unharvested, un-made-into-jam.
Maybe I should feel guilty.

I don't.

Making Room For Science

Perhaps God fashioned us
from dust, whispers, and mystery.

Or perhaps the sea formed us
from saline, sand, and memory
before God knew what he was doing.

God As Screenwriter

It's not like him
to direct, to tell us
where to stand or
what to say.

He frames a story,
remains off set,
leaves directing
to the angels—

who urge us,
actors of our lives,
toward unlimited
artistic license.

Maybe This Is Heaven

When you live with people for
twelve years in schoolrooms,
lunchrooms, football fields,
choral chambers, locker rooms—

when you know who got
her period first, who was
picked last for kickball and
who wasn't invited to prom

and you remember the sound of
your friend's laugh when he was
seventeen because at forty-five
he still has that voice but deeper

when you all meet unexpectedly in
your hometown and even though
you look like your parents now
you relax into conversation

like you were never gone
like nothing has changed and
the world is still young and kind—
how you imagine it might be again.

I Dreamed A Question:

What Happens When We Die?

Swim, he said,
push off the bottom of
the-hundred-foot-deep,
leave your seal suit behind
and come find us.

Swim, she said,
up toward the light,
break the surface,
take a breath
and fly home.

Music and Silence

Today I caught a glimpse of
invisible strings strung between
  lovers,
stretched tight, tuned to each other
through years and moments of living.

I heard sympathetic vibrations in
an old woman's fingers woven
between her husband's when he died.
This is why we fear Love:

the music
the silence.

I sleep beneath a quilt

and dream of cotton, lace, silk,
of women's hands held just-so,
the needle set, thread pulled
through beeswax, over tongue,
stitches sung while women sew
memories. I sleep beneath
music made by women's hands,
dream beneath a quilt made by
my grandmothers and while I sleep
they lay their needles down and
touch my feet. They lay their quilted
hands on my head, heart, belly
breast and bless me. What is
the garment of God's love if
not a quilt, a blanket blessing
from the hands who made it?
Who dressed us when we left the
garden? Who made the skins
we wear? I dream beneath a quilt
sung by the Mother, her music
weaving sunrise through darkness,
her wisdom warming me with
mystery, enfolding me in light.

I Tell My Children

If you want to know me, look in here.
There will be no other record after I'm gone—
in place of ashes, I leave these slim cardboard volumes

these and the songs I sang to you at bedtime,
melodies I hummed while stirring vegetable soup
late at night with the first autumn cold snap.

You will not find me bound in tidy brown leather,
gold leaf lettering the cover, nor embellished
with stickers on acid-free paper.

I will be faded to almost nothing where I wrote in pencil.

When you read, you may hear my alto or perhaps
remember the way my freckled hands turned pages.
You may discover a blossom pressed where it fell

unnoticed from the wisteria one summer.
Remember how it grew in braids up the ancient Cedar
by the corner of the house; how in early morning

while you slept, I sat beneath walnut trees,
writing about robins digging worms in rain-soaked soil,
a crescent moon at daybreak?

You will find me recalling a certain sunset,
Lauren's golden hair, Sara tasting ocean sand,
the smell of Luke when he was seven.

If you look, you will find me here—
quiet in the hammock, the apple I was eating
fallen to the ground unfinished.

Missing God

I don't remember
her voice.

But sometimes
in the mountains
I think I hear
an echo

of the flute
she played.

Words

the older I get the fewer I need—
infant tongue returns and
through pursed lips I want
only to taste the world
in silence and
remember.

Acknowledgments

Sincere thanks to the editors who first published these poems, some in slightly different versions:

Irreantum: Fish Bones
Seasons of Change, Stories of Transition from Segullah Writers:
    Coming Up For Air, I Tell My Children,
Last Night I Prayed
Segullah: Be Still, I Sleep Beneath A Quilt, Law of the Harvest
Utah Sings, Volume VIII: Chrysalis, Missing God
Utah Voices 2012: Winter Heard Me Call Your Name

Special thanks to Fae Ellsworth, who lovingly and relentlessly urged me toward completion of this manuscript, to Twila Newey, Dalene Rowley, Rynell Lewis, Jason Kerr, and MaryJan Munger for early editorial feedback and to the wonderful BCC Press team for bringing this collection to print. Thanks to the members of Word Weavers, a chapter of Utah State Poetry Society, who read early drafts of several of these poems many years ago during gatherings in warm and delightful homes of the various Keith Sisters: Mary, Karen, and Helen. Eternal gratitude to my family of origin: Twila, Sylvia, Lance, Jean, Von, and Whitney, for inspiring and infusing my world with hope. Thanks, most of all, to my Jeffrey.

MELODY NEWEY JOHNSON was born in Baltimore, Maryland, and spent most of her growing-up years in Utah, where she currently resides with her spouse. Her award-winning poems have been published online and in print literary journals and anthologies, including *Dialogue: A Journal of Mormon Thought, Exponent II, Irreantum, Psaltry & Lyre, Segullah, Utah Voices 2012, Utah Sings, Vol. VIII* and elsewhere. Her work has also appeared in collaborative art exhibits in Salt Lake City. She has been featured in Poetry in The Garden at Red Butte Garden and at Artists of Utah's 15 Bytes. She is a past poetry editor for *Exponent II* magazine and current poetry editor for *Segullah* journal. She is the creator of Living Well: Retreat to Self, a women's writing retreat. She earns a living as a Registered Nurse and lives to write. This is her first full length manuscript.

Made in the USA
Monee, IL
21 July 2020